HEALTH FOR LIFE

low-fat

JODY VASSALLO

FORTIORI

WHAT'S SO IMPORTANT ABOUT A LOW-FAT DIET?

A certain amount of fat is needed for good health, but eating too much fat can cause health problems. Fatty foods contain more calories than equal-weight portions of low-fat foods and tend to be less filling. So a high-fat diet makes it much easier to eat more calories than are necessary and to gain weight, which in turn increases the risk of developing diabetes and other health problems. High-fat diets are also associated with an increased risk of certain cancers, particularly if fruit and vegetables are not eaten regularly. Eating too much saturated fat can raise blood cholesterol in children and adults, increasing the risk of developing heart disease, which remains a major cause of death. In fact, saturated fat can increase blood cholesterol to a greater extent than dietary cholesterol. Eating too much saturated fat can also impair the body's ability to respond to the hormone insulin, which increases the risk of developing type 2 diabetes, particularly if you are overweight.

BUILDING A LOW-FAT DIET

Eating a healthy low-fat diet and having an active lifestyle will make you look good, feel great and help prevent future health problems. High-fat diets cause health problems due to the metabolic effects of excess fat and also because they don't contain enough of the most nutritious foods. You should be able to get your fat intake to a healthy level simply by eating more healthy foods and less fatty and processed foods. Basing your diet on the well-known pyramid model is an easy way to eat a healthy, balanced low-fat diet and should satisfy the largest appetite. Even better, the more you fill up on healthy, nutritious foods the less you will crave 'junk' foods, particularly if you're active.

THE FOUR MAIN TYPES OF FAT FOUND IN FOODS

1 | **Saturated fat** when consumed in relatively large amounts causes the liver to make more cholesterol, which raises blood cholesterol and increases the risk of heart disease. Foods rich in saturated fat include full-fat dairy products, lard, fatty meats and poultry, and foods fried in palm oil. It is also hidden in many processed and fast foods like biscuits, cakes, pastries and a range of common snack foods.

2 | **Monounsaturated fat** when consumed in moderation can help lower blood cholesterol, if your total and saturated fat intake is low. Good sources include olive and canola oils, monounsaturated margarine, avocado and macadamia nuts.

3 | **Polyunsaturated fat** can help lower blood cholesterol, if your diet is low in total and saturated fat. There are two types of polyunsaturated fat that cannot be made in the body and must be obtained from foods – omega-3 and omega-6 essential fats. A good balance of these is needed in the diet for the proper functioning of many important bodily processes such as blood clotting, and controlling inflammation and blood pressure. Most people eat too much omega-6 fat. Good sources of omega-3 fat include canola and linseed oils, walnuts, omega-3-enriched eggs, and oily fish (tuna, salmon, mackerel, trout). Foods with omega-6 fat include sunflower oil, safflower oil, polyunsaturated spreads and sunflower seeds.

4 | **Trans fatty acids** are fats that are mostly made when liquid vegetable oils are turned into a semi-solid form to make vegetable shortening or margarine. Eating a lot of these can increase 'bad' LDL-cholesterol and decrease 'good' HDL-cholesterol levels in your blood, increasing the risk of heart disease. Check food labels to avoid products containing partially hydrogenated or hydrogenated oil/fat such as biscuits, packet cakes, pastries, coffee creamers and snack foods.

HOW MUCH FAT IS HEALTHY?

For healthy adults and teenagers, health authorities recommend that no more than 30% of the daily energy intake (measured in calories/kilojoules) comes from fat (monounsaturated 13%, polyunsaturated 10% and saturated 7%). On average, this amounts to no more than 50–80 grams of fat per day for men and 40-60 grams of fat per day for women. Generally, main meals should contain less than 15-20 grams of fat and snacks less than 5 grams of fat. However, individual fat requirements may vary depending on health, body size and activity level. Check with your doctor to confirm that a low-fat diet is safe for you. It will probably be recommended if you are overweight or have high blood cholesterol, or if you have a family history of either heart disease or diabetes.

A HEALTHY LOW-FAT DIET

1 | **EAT MOST: vegetables, fruit, wholegrain bread and cereal products, legumes**
Main meals and snacks should be based on these foods, because they are low in fat but rich in vitamins, minerals, antioxidants, fibre and carbohydrate energy. Filling up on them will provide more healthy nutrients but less fat and calories per mouthful – essential for healthy weight control. Aim to eat a variety of different coloured fruits and vegetables each day.

2 | **DRINK MOST: plain water**

3 | **EAT IN MODERATION: lean meat and poultry, fish, seafood, eggs, low-fat dairy or soy products, nuts and seeds**
These foods are rich in protein and contain many beneficial vitamins and minerals.

Some can be high in fat, so choose low- or reduced-fat dairy products, lean cuts of meat and poultry, and use low-fat cooking methods. Because many people don't eat enough iron, zinc and omega-3 fat, health experts recommend that we eat lean red meat 3-4 times each week, but not in large portions. Limit yourself to palm-sized portions of meat and poultry and satisfy your appetite with vegetables and grains.

4 | EAT & DRINK LEAST: fats and oils, salt, sugar and sugary foods or drinks, 'junk' foods, fried foods, alcohol

These foods should not be regularly eaten because they contain many calories but few vitamins or minerals. If you consume a lot of these, it is likely that your health will eventually suffer. When reaching for a treat, consider making a healthier choice.

LOW-FAT FAST FOOD

There will be times when you're away from home or too tired to cook, and on the lookout for fast food. By choosing carefully, you will find nutritious food that's not too high in fat. Pastries, pies and battered or fried foods are high in fat and best avoided. If you're dining out, you can ask which menu items are low-fat, or whether a low-fat dish can be specially prepared for you. Most food halls have a variety of outlets, with a range of nutritious low-fat options such as sushi, vegetable soup, salad rolls or stir fried dishes.

HOW TO EAT LESS FAT

1 | Choose low- or reduced-fat dairy or alternative products (such as soy) instead of full-fat ones.

2 | Reduce the amount of margarine and butter you use and switch to reduced-fat canola- or olive oil-based spreads.

3 | Instead of butter, lard or shortening, use stock, or canola or olive oil, for cooking.

4 | Choose lean meat cuts, skinless poultry trimmed of any visible fat, and fish canned in brine or spring water instead of oil.

5 | Use low-fat tomato- and vegetable-based sauces instead of cheese or cream-based sauces.

6 | Replace full-fat mayonnaise and oily dressings with fat-free dressings, lemon juice or flavoured vinegar.

7 | Choose low-fat snacks such as rice crackers, low-fat pretzels, rice cakes, no-fat microwave popcorn, fruit, vegetables or low-fat yoghurt instead of chips, biscuits, chocolates and other fatty foods.

8 | Use low fat cooking methods such as steaming, microwaving, stir frying and dry-frying in a non-stick pan.

9 | Read the nutrition information on food labels to help you select low-fat foods.

10 | Keep your fridge, freezer and pantry well-stocked with healthy low-fat foods (see overleaf). Having healthy foods on hand makes it much easier to stick with a healthy, low-fat diet.

Dr Susanna Holt
(PhD and registered dietitian)

A HEALTHY PANTRY

dried fruit

low-fat yoghurt

low-fat crackers

canned & dried legum

low-fat ice cream

fresh fruit

low-fat milks

lean chicken

fruit in natural juice

omega-3 eggs

fresh fish

low-fat bakery goo

Stock up on these foods for a healthy pantry: Low-fat versions of cereal & grain products breakfast cereals and bars, fruit loaf, crumpets, muffins, grainy bread & rolls, bagels, pita bread, crackers, pizza bases, pasta, noodles, rice, barley, couscous, polenta, meat-filled tortellini & ravioli, canned spaghetti, pretzels, microwave popcorn, muffin and pancake mixes **Vegetables & fruit** raw or lightly cooked fresh, or canned or frozen, vegetables; frozen thick-cut low-fat oven-bake chips, vegetable juice, fresh, frozen & dried fruit, fruit in natural juice or juice with no added sugar **Low- or reduced-fat dairy products or alternatives (soy or rice milk)**

lean meats

olive oil

fresh vegetables

low-fat cheddar cheese

educed-fat spreads

pasta, rice & noodles

low fat pizza bases

tomato pasta sauces

ats & natural muesli

frozen vegetables

reduced-fat white cheeses

tuna in brine or water

milk, fresh or frozen yoghurt, custard, cottage & ricotta cheese. **Meat, poultry, eggs and fish** lean red meat, low-fat mince, skinless chicken or turkey, omega-3-enriched eggs, fresh or frozen plain fish fillets, fish canned in brine or spring water **Legumes, nuts and seeds** dried, canned or vacuum-packed legumes, baked beans, soy burgers, tempeh, tofu, unsalted raw nuts, sunflower seeds, pepitas **Condiments, spreads, seasonings and oils** bottled tomato pasta sauce, dried or fresh herbs, garlic, ginger, spices, no-fat dressings or mayonnaise, vinegar, lemon, stock, Vegemite, jam, honey, reduced-fat margarine, olive oil or canola cooking sprays

BREAKFAST

soft eggs with ham soldiers

SOFT EGGS WITH HAM SOLDIERS

4 thick slices (170 g/5²/3 oz) wholegrain bread

4 slices (100 g/3¹/3 oz) 97% fat-free ham

12 chives

olive oil spray

4 eggs*

1 Trim the crusts from the bread and discard. Cut each slice into 3 even soldiers.

2 Cut the ham into strips as wide as the bread and place on top of the bread. Wrap a chive around each soldier. Spray both sides of the bread lightly with olive oil spray.

3 Cook the soldiers, bread side up, under a grill preheated to medium until crisp and golden.

4 Put the eggs into a pan of cold water and slowly bring to the boil. Gently boil for 3 minutes. Transfer to egg cups, cut off the tops and serve with soldiers to the side. Serves 4

per serve I fat 8 g I protein 15 g I carbohydrate 18.5 g I fibre 2 g I cholesterol 200.5 mg I energy 865 kj (205 cal)
*Choosing omega-3 fat-enriched eggs increases the amount of beneficial omega-3 fat in this recipe.

PEPITA PORRIDGE WITH MIXED BERRIES

2 cups (190 g/6¹/4 oz) quick-cook oats

2 tablespoons oat bran

50 g (1²/3 oz) pepitas (edible pumpkin seeds)

200 ml (6¹/2 fl oz) reduced-fat Greek-style yoghurt

300 g (10 oz) fresh or frozen mixed berries

2 tablespoons soft brown sugar

skim or no-fat milk, to serve

1 Put the oats, bran and pepitas into a pan. Add 4 cups (1 litre/32 fl oz) water and cook, stirring constantly, over a medium heat for 3-5 minutes or until the oats are soft and creamy.

2 Divide the porridge among 4 bowls, top with a generous dollop of yoghurt, some mixed berries and sprinkled brown sugar.

3 Serve the milk to the side. Serves 4

per serve (not including milk) I fat 11 g I protein 13 g I carbohydrate 46.5 g I fibre 7 g I cholesterol 5 mg I energy 1420 kj (340 cal)

pepita porridge with mixed berries

balsamic mushrooms & tomatoes on toast

BALSAMIC MUSHROOMS & TOMATOES ON TOAST

1 Lightly spray the mushrooms and tomatoes with olive oil spray and place onto a foil-lined grill tray. Cook under a preheated grill on high for 5 minutes on each side, or until the mushrooms are brown and tender. Drizzle with the balsamic vinegar.

2 Put the ricotta and basil into a bowl and mix gently to combine.

3 Toast the bread and spread one side of each slice with the ricotta mixture.

4 Top with tomatoes and mushrooms and finish with some cracked black pepper. Put the rocket and parmesan into a bowl, toss to combine and serve on the side. Serves 4

per serve I fat 9.5 g I protein 17 g I carbohydrate 39 g I fibre 6 g I cholesterol 22.5 mg I energy 1305 kj (310 cal)

8 (150 g/5 oz) field (flat) mushrooms

200 g (6½ oz) cherry tomatoes on the vine, 170 g (5²/3 oz) edible weight

olive oil spray

3 tablespoons balsamic vinegar

100 g (3⅓ oz) low-fat ricotta cheese

2 tablespoons finely shredded fresh basil

8 thick slices (345 g/11⅓ oz) wholegrain bread

cracked black pepper

50 g (1²/3 oz) baby rocket (arugula)

50 g (1²/3 oz) parmesan cheese, shaved

smoked salmon & eggs with caper yoghurt mayo

SMOKED SALMON & EGGS WITH CAPER YOGHURT MAYO

1 Crack the eggs into a large fry pan half-filled with water and cook in barely simmering water until the eggs are done to your liking. Soft-centered eggs will take about 2-3 minutes. Remove and drain on absorbent paper.
2 Toast the bagels until crisp and golden, top with spinach, smoked salmon and eggs.
3 Whisk together the capers and yoghurt and spoon over the eggs. Serves 4

per serve | **fat 7.5 g** | **protein 22 g** | **carbohydrate 34.5 g** | **fibre 4.5 g** | **cholesterol 202 mg** | **energy 1235 kj (295 cal)**

4 eggs
4 (280 g/9 oz) wholegrain
   bagels, split in half
100 g (3⅓ oz) baby spinach
100 g (3⅓ oz) smoked salmon
2 tablespoons chopped capers
3 tablespoons reduced-fat
   plain yoghurt

FRUIT FINGERS WITH PASSIONFRUIT YOGHURT DIP

1 Cut the fruit into 2.5 cm (1 in) thick, long fingers. Arrange in glasses.
2 Put the yoghurt, passionfruit pulp and maple syrup into a bowl and mix to combine.
3 Serve the fruit with individual pots of the dip and muesli to the side. Serves 4

per serve | **fat 1.5 g** | **protein 8 g** | **carbohydrate 40.5 g** | **fibre 9 g** | **cholesterol 3 mg** | **energy 875 kj (210 cal)**

300 g (10 oz) peeled
   red papaya
2 (200 g/6½ oz) bananas
300 g (10 oz) peeled
   rockmelon
300 g (10 oz) peeled
   pineapple
1 cup (250 ml/8 fl oz)
   low-fat plain yoghurt
¼ cup (60 ml/2 fl oz)
   passionfruit pulp
1 tablespoon maple syrup
½ cup (50 g/1⅔ oz)
   natural muesli

fruit fingers with passionfruit yoghurt dip

cinnamon sugar crumpets with banana

CINNAMON SUGAR CRUMPETS WITH BANANA

4 (180 g/6 oz) wholemeal
   crumpets
2 eggs, lightly beaten
1 cup (250 ml/8 fl oz) skim
   or no-fat milk
1 teaspoon ground cinnamon
3 tablespoons caster sugar
4 (475 g/15 oz) sugar bananas

1 Whisk together the eggs and milk.

2 Dip the crumpets one at a time into the egg mixture, allowing any excess to drain off.

3 Cook the crumpets in a non-stick fry pan over medium heat for about 2 minutes or until golden brown on both sides.

4 Coat both sides of each cooked crumpet in the combined cinnamon and sugar.

5 Serve the crumpets with sliced banana. Serves 4

per serve | fat 3 g | protein 10 g | carbohydrate 63.5 g | fibre 6.5 g | cholesterol 95.5 mg | energy 1345 kj (320 cal)

VANILLA BLUEBERRY PANCAKES

2 cups (250 g/8 oz)
   self-raising flour
1/3 cup (90 g/3 oz) caster sugar
2 eggs, lightly beaten
80 g (2²/3 oz) reduced-fat
   polyunsaturated margarine
300 ml (10 fl oz) skim
   or no-fat milk
1 teaspoon vanilla essence
2 cups (310 g/10¹/3 oz) fresh
   or frozen blueberries
canola oil spray
maple syrup to serve

1 Sift the flour into a bowl and stir in the sugar. Make a well in the center.

2 Whisk together the egg, melted margarine, milk and vanilla. Pour into the well and whisk until smooth. Gently fold through the blueberries.

3 Lightly spray a non-stick fry pan with canola oil spray. Pour 1/4 cup (60 ml/2 fl oz) of the batter into the pan and cook over low heat for 3 minutes or until bubbles appear and pop on the surface.

4 Turn the pancake over and cook the other side until golden. Keep warm and continue with the rest of the mixture. Serve stacks of pancakes drizzled with maple syrup. Makes 8 pancakes (serves 4)

per serve | fat 11.5 g | protein 13.5 g | carbohydrate 84.5 g | fibre 4 g | cholesterol 96 mg | energy 2070 kj (495 cal)

vanilla blueberry pancakes

RASPBERRY, BANANA & BRAN MUFFINS

2½ cups (315 g/10½ oz)
self-raising flour

1 teaspoon baking powder

1 teaspoon mixed spice

1 cup (40 g/1⅓ oz) bran
flakes cereal *oat bran cereal.*

½ cup (115 g/3⅔ oz) firmly
packed brown sugar

1 cup (125 g/4 oz) frozen
raspberries *(strawberries)*

½ cup (125 g/4 oz) mashed
banana *milk + vinegar*

1 cup (250 ml/8 fl oz) buttermilk

1 egg, lightly beaten

½ cup (125 g/4 oz) low-fat
ricotta cheese

1 tablespoon light olive oil

1 Lightly grease 6 x ⅓ cup (80 ml/2⅔ fl oz) capacity muffin holes.

2 Sift the flour, baking powder and mixed spice into a bowl. Stir in the bran flakes and brown sugar. Carefully fold through the raspberries. Make a well in the center of the ingredients.

3 Whisk together the banana, buttermilk, egg, ricotta and olive oil and pour into the well.

4 Gently fold the mixture until just combined. Do not over mix or the texture will be rubbery.

5 Divide the mixture evenly among the muffin holes. Bake for 20 minutes or until the muffins are puffed and golden and begin to come away from the sides of the pan.

6 Allow to cool for a couple of minutes in the pan before turning out on a wire rack to cool. Makes 6

per muffin | fat 7.5 g | protein 12 g | carbohydrate 72.5 g | fibre 5 g | cholesterol 44 mg | energy 1700 kj (405 cal)

raspberry, banana & bran muffins

SOUPS & SNACKS

creamy pumpkin & lima bean soup

CREAMY PUMPKIN & LIMA BEAN SOUP

200 g (6½ oz) dried lima beans,
    soaked in cold water overnight
2 teaspoons olive oil
1 medium brown onion,
    finely chopped
1 kg (2 lb) peeled Jap or butternut
    pumpkin, roughly chopped
pinch nutmeg
4 cups (1 litre/32 fl oz)
    reduced-salt chicken stock
¾ cup (75 g/2½ oz) skim
    milk powder
chervil sprigs to garnish

1 Rinse the lima beans under cold water. Simmer the beans in a large pan of water for 40 minutes or until soft. Drain and remove any loose skins.

2 Heat the oil in a large pan, add the onion and cook over medium heat for 3 minutes or until golden. Add the pumpkin and nutmeg and cook, stirring occasionally, for 5 minutes more.

3 Add the chicken stock, bring to the boil, reduce heat and simmer for 30 minutes or until the pumpkin is soft. Stir in the milk powder. Remove from the heat, add the cooked beans and set aside to cool slightly.

4 Puree the soup in batches until smooth and creamy. Garnish with chervil sprigs. Serves 6

per serve | fat 3.5 g | protein 17.5 g | carbohydrate 32 g | fibre 6 g | cholesterol 4 mg | energy 940 kj (225 cal)

ROASTED GARLIC, TOMATO & BASIL SOUP

3 medium heads garlic, whole
1 kg (2 lb) Roma tomatoes,
    halved lengthwise
1 medium brown onion, halved
cracked black pepper
4 cups (1 litre/32 fl oz)
    reduced-salt vegetable stock
2 teaspoons sugar
2 tablespoons finely shredded
    fresh basil

1 Preheat oven to 180°C (350°F/Gas 4).

2 Put the garlic, tomatoes and onion onto a baking tray lined with baking paper. Sprinkle with cracked black pepper and bake for 40 minutes or until the tomatoes are soft.

3 Remove the skins from the garlic and discard.

4 Roughly chop the tomatoes, reserving any juice.

5 Put the garlic, tomato and onion into a food processor and process until smooth. Transfer to a pan, stir in the stock, sugar and basil and cook over medium heat for 5 minutes or until the soup is heated through. Serves 4

per serve | fat 1.5 g | protein 6.5 g | carbohydrate 11.5 g | fibre 5.5 g | cholesterol 0 mg | energy 375 kj (90 cal)

roasted garlic, tomato & basil soup

easy tofu & vegetable laksa

EASY TOFU & VEGETABLE LAKSA

1 Put the vermicelli into a bowl, cover with boiling water and allow to stand for 10 minutes or until the noodles are soft. Rinse and drain well.

2 Pour the coconut milk into a wok, add the laksa paste and cook over medium heat for 5 minutes or until fragrant.

3 Add the stock and tofu puffs and simmer for 10 minutes. Add the vegetables and palm sugar and cook for 5 minutes more or until tender.

4 Divide the noodles among the serving bowls, ladle the soup over and serve topped with bean sprouts and coriander leaves. Serves 6

per serve I **fat 7 g** I **protein 7.5 g** I **carbohydrate 22.5 g** I **fibre 3.5 g** I **cholesterol 0 mg** I **energy 775 kj (185 cal)**

100 g (3$\frac{1}{3}$ oz) dried rice vermicelli
275 ml (9 fl oz) reduced-fat
    coconut milk
2 tablespoons laksa paste
6 cups (1.5 litres/48 fl oz)
    reduced-salt vegetable stock
8 (80 g/2$\frac{2}{3}$ oz) tofu puffs, halved
100 g (3$\frac{1}{3}$ oz) baby corn,
    halved lengthwise
100 g (3$\frac{1}{3}$ oz) snowpeas
1 bunch (225 g/7 oz) baby
    bok choy, roughly chopped
1 medium tomato, cut into
    wedges
1 tablespoon grated palm sugar
    or brown sugar
50 g (1$\frac{2}{3}$ oz) bean sprouts
$\frac{1}{4}$ cup fresh coriander (cilantro)
    leaves

pumpkin hummus with bagel toast

PUMPKIN HUMMUS WITH BAGEL TOAST

1 Preheat oven to 200°C (400°F/Gas 6).
2 Put the pumpkin onto a baking tray, spray with olive oil spray and cook for 30 minutes or until soft.
3 Put the chickpeas and pumpkin into a food processor. Add the lemon juice, cumin and garlic and process until smooth and creamy.
4 Cut the bagels through the center into wafer thin slices. Spray lightly with olive oil spray and bake for 15-20 minutes or until crisp and golden. Serves 4
per serve | fat 3.5 g | protein 13 g | carbohydrate 41.5 g | fibre 7.5 g | cholesterol 0 mg | energy 1040 kj (250 cal)

300 g (10 oz) peeled pumpkin,
    cut into 1cm (½ in) slices
olive oil spray
400 g (13 oz) can chickpeas,
    rinsed and drained
    weight 300 g (10 oz)
1 tablespoon lemon juice
½ teaspoon ground cumin
2 cloves garlic, chopped
4 (220 g/7 oz) wholegrain bagels

MOROCCAN CHICKEN & TOMATO SOUP

1 Heat the oil in a large pan, add the spices and chicken and cook over medium heat for 5 minutes or until the chicken is golden.
2 Add the spring onions and parsley and cook for 2 minutes more.
3 Stir in the tomatoes and stock, bring to the boil, reduce heat and simmer for 15 minutes.
4 Remove from the heat and add the couscous and spinach. Cover and allow to stand for 10 minutes. Stir well before serving. Serves 4
per serve | fat 13 g | protein 31.5 g | carbohydrate 25.5 g | fibre 4 g | cholesterol 108.5 mg | energy 1430 kj (340 cal)

2 teaspoons olive oil
2 teaspoons ground turmeric
2 teaspoons ground cumin
500 g (1 lb) skinless chicken
    thigh fillets, chopped
4 spring onions (scallions),
    finely sliced
½ cup (15 g/½ oz) fresh
    flat-leaf parsley, chopped
400 g (13 oz) can chopped
    tomatoes
4 cups (1 litre/32 fl oz)
    reduced-salt chicken stock
½ cup (90 g/3 oz) couscous
200 g (6½ oz) English
    spinach, finely shredded

moroccan chicken & tomato soup

soy honey chicken nuggets with plum sauce

SOY HONEY CHICKEN NUGGETS WITH PLUM SAUCE

500g (1 lb) skinless chicken
    breast meat
1 tablespoon honey
2 tablespoons reduced-salt
    soy sauce
1 clove garlic, crushed
1 egg white
2 cups (60 g/2 oz) cornflakes,
    crushed
1 tablespoon sesame seeds
¼ cup (60 ml/2 fl oz) plum sauce
1 tablespoon rice vinegar

1 Preheat oven to 200°C (400°F/Gas 6).
2 Cut the chicken into bite-size pieces. Whisk together the honey, soy, garlic and egg white in a shallow non-metallic bowl. Add chicken and marinate in the fridge for 30 minutes.
3 Remove the chicken from the marinade and coat in the combined cornflake crumbs and sesame seeds. Bake on a baking tray lined with baking paper for 10-15 minutes or until the chicken is tender.
4 Whisk together the plum sauce and vinegar. Serve the chicken nuggets with the plum dipping sauce to the side. Serves 6

per serve | fat 6 g | protein 20 g | carbohydrate 19 g | fibre 0.5 g | cholesterol 55 mg | energy 865 kj (205 cal)

SWEET CHILLI POPCORN RICE SNACK

2 teaspoons olive oil
½ cup (100 g/3⅓ oz) uncooked
    popping corn
100 g (3⅓ oz) rice crackers
2 tablespoons sweet chilli sauce

1 Put the oil and popping corn into a large pan, cover tightly and cook over medium heat for 3-5 minutes, shaking the pan occasionally once the corn starts to pop.
2 Transfer popcorn to a large bowl and add the rice crackers. Drizzle over sweet chilli and toss to coat in the sauce. Serve immediately. Serves 6

per serve | fat 3.5 g | protein 4 g | carbohydrate 28.5 g | fibre 6 g | cholesterol 0 mg | energy 685 kj (165 cal)

sweet chilli popcorn rice snack

TUNA SUSHI WEDGES

1 cup (205 g/8 oz) short-grain rice

2 tablespoons seasoned rice
   vinegar

400 g (13 oz) can tuna in water,
   drained weight 280 g (9 oz)

3 spring onions (scallions), sliced

1 tablespoon finely shredded
   pickled ginger

2 tablespoons low-fat mayonnaise

4 (20 g/²/₃ oz) sheets nori
   seaweed

20 g (²/₃ oz) baby spinach

1 Put the rice into a pan and cover with 1 cup (250 ml/8 fl oz) cold water. Bring to the boil and cook for 10 minutes or until tunnels start to appear on the surface of the rice. Reduce heat to low, cover and cook for 10 minutes or until rice is soft.
2 Stir the vinegar into the hot rice. Spread out on a baking tray and set aside to cool.
3 Put the tuna, spring onions, pickled ginger and mayonnaise into a bowl and mix to combine.
4 Lay out one half of nori shiny-side down onto a chopping board. Spread a 1 cm (¹/₂ in) thick layer of rice over the nori sheet. Cut in half diagonally.
5 Lay a couple of spinach leaves across the rice on one sheet and top with 1-2 tablespoons of the tuna mixture. Fold the nori over to form a triangle. Cut in half and serve with salad. Serves 4

per serve I **fat 3.5 g** I **protein 22.5 g** I **carbohydrate 44 g** I **fibre 5 g** I **cholesterol 39 mg** I **energy 1265 kj (300 cal)**

tuna sushi wedges

chicken & corn noodle bites

CHICKEN & CORN NOODLE BITES

1 Lightly spray 8 egg rings with olive oil spray.
2 Cook the noodles in boiling water for 2-3 minutes or until tender. Drain well.
3 Put the egg rings into a lightly olive oil sprayed, large non-stick fry pan. Divide the noodles among the egg rings and fill with a little each of the chicken, corn and spring onion.
4 Whisk the eggs, milk and cheese together in a jug. Pour into the rings and cook over low-medium heat for 5-10 minutes then turn over and cook the other side until golden and cooked. Serves 8

per serve I fat 5.5 g I protein 10 g I carbohydrate 7.5 g I fibre 1 g I cholesterol 72 mg I energy 500 kj (120 cal)

olive oil spray
50 g (1²/₃ oz) instant noodles
1 cup (180 g/6 oz) shredded, skinless barbecue chicken,
130 g (4 oz) can corn kernels, drained weight 90 g (3 oz)
2 spring onions (scallions), sliced
2 eggs, lightly beaten
½ cup (125 ml/4 fl oz) skim or no-fat milk
30 g (1 oz) parmesan cheese, finely grated

PEA, POTATO & HAM SOUP

2 teaspoons olive oil

1 medium leek, washed and
  thinly sliced crosswise

125 g (4 oz) 97% fat-free ham,
  chopped

750 g (1½ lb) peeled potatoes,
  chopped

5 cups (1.25 litres/40 fl oz)
  reduced-salt chicken stock

1 cup (150 g/5 oz) fresh
  or frozen peas

salt and pepper

1 Heat the oil in a large pan, add the leek and ham and cook over medium heat for 5 minutes or until the leek is soft.

2 Add the potatoes and stock and bring to the boil. Reduce heat and simmer for 30 minutes or until the potatoes are tender.

3 Stir in the peas and cook for 5 minutes more or until soft. Season to taste with salt and pepper. Serves 6

per serve I **fat 3.5 g** I **protein 11 g** I **carbohydrate 21 g** I **fibre 4 g** I **cholesterol 11 mg** I **energy 680 kj (165 cal)**

pea, potato & ham soup

LUNCH

lunchbox noodles

LUNCHBOX NOODLES

575 g (1 lb 2 oz) skinless
  chicken breasts
1 lime, sliced
250 g (8 oz) 98% fat-free
  Hokkien noodles
3 spring onions (scallions), sliced
200 g (6½ oz) baby green
  beans, steamed
250 g (8 oz) asparagus, halved
  lengthwise and steamed
1 carrot, sliced
2 tomatoes, cut into thin wedges
¼ cup coriander (cilantro) leaves
3 tablespoons lime juice
1 tablespoon fish sauce
3 tablespoons sweet chilli sauce
1 teaspoon sesame oil

1 Put the chicken breasts into a deep fry pan, cover with water, add the lime slices and cook over low heat for 15 minutes or until the chicken is tender. Cool slightly in the water, then cut into thin strips.
2 Put noodles into a bowl, cover with boiling water and stand for 3 minutes or until tender, then drain.
3 Toss together the spring onions, beans, asparagus, carrot, tomato and coriander.
4 Arrange the noodles in a lunchbox and top with vegetables and chicken.
5 Whisk together the lime juice, fish sauce, sweet chilli and sesame oil. Pour the dressing over the salad just before serving. Serves 4

per serve | fat 10.5 g | protein 41 g | carbohydrate 41 g | fibre 6 g | cholesterol 103 mg | energy 1790 kj (425 cal)

SALMON PAN BAGNA

4 (300 g/10 oz) long, crusty
  wholegrain rolls
2 Roma tomatoes, sliced
1 red (Spanish) onion, sliced
1 clove garlic, crushed
2 tablespoons red wine vinegar
2 teaspoons extra virgin olive oil
2 hard-boiled eggs, sliced
75 g (2½ oz) can pink salmon
  in spring water, drained
  weight 60 g (2 oz)
2 tablespoons capers, drained
½ medium green capsicum (bell
  pepper), thinly sliced

1 Cut the rolls in half lengthwise. Put the tomatoes and onion in a shallow bowl. Whisk together the garlic, vinegar and olive oil in a jug and pour over the tomatoes. Leave mixture to combine for 10 minutes.
2 Fill the rolls with eggs, salmon, capers, capsicum and prepared tomato and onion mixture. Wrap each roll tightly in foil and weigh down on a tray in the fridge for 1 hour. Serves 4

per serve | fat 9 g | protein 14.5 g | carbohydrate 40 g | fibre 5.5 g | cholesterol 120 mg | energy 1260 kj (300 cal)

salmon pan bagna

speedy nachos

SPEEDY NACHOS

1 Put the beans and sweet chilli sauce into a pan and bring to the boil. Remove from the heat and divide the beans among 4 individual pots.
2 Divide the corn chips among 4 shallow heatproof dishes and sprinkle with grated cheese. Cook under a preheated grill on medium until the cheese is golden and bubbling.
3 Put the capsicum, halved tomatoes, avocado and lime juice into a bowl and mix to combine. Season with cracked black pepper. Gently fold through the coriander leaves.
4 Serve pots of beans with the corn chips and salsa to the side. Serves 4

per serve I fat 14 g I protein 12 g I carbohydrate 29 g I fibre 10 g I cholesterol 7 mg I energy 1230 kj (295 cal)

400 g (13 oz) can chilli red kidney
  beans, drained weight
  300 g (10 oz)
1 tablespoon sweet chilli sauce
100 g (3¹/₃ oz) toasted light
  corn chips
50 g (1²/₃ oz) reduced-fat
  cheddar cheese, finely grated
1 medium green capsicum
  (bell pepper), chopped
200 g (6¹/₂ oz) cherry tomatoes
¹/₂ (125 g/4 oz) avocado, chopped
1 tablespoon lime juice
cracked black pepper
1 tablespoon fresh coriander
  (cilantro) leaves

CARAMELISED ONION, ARTICHOKE & TOMATO PIZZAS

1 Preheat oven to 200°C (400°F/Gas 6).
2 Heat the oil in a large fry pan, add the onions and balsamic and cook over a medium heat for 10-15 minutes or until the onions caramelise.
3 Spread tomato paste over the pizza bases and top with caramelised onion. Evenly distribute the tomato, artichoke and olives. Bake for 10 minutes or until the bases are crisp and golden.
4 Scatter with the rocket and fetta. Serves 4

per serve I fat 9.5 g I protein 19 g I carbohydrate 76.5 g I fibre 11 g I cholesterol 8.5 mg I energy 1725 kj (410 cal)

2 teaspoons olive oil
4 medium brown onions,
  thinly sliced
2 tablespoons balsamic vinegar
2 tablespoons tomato paste
4 (450 g/15 oz) individual 96%
  fat-free pizza bases
75 g (2¹/₂ oz) semi-dried
  tomatoes, thinly sliced
400 g (13 oz) can artichoke
  hearts, drained weight
  300 g (10 oz), sliced
12 kalamata olives
30 g (1 oz) baby rocket (arugula)
50 g (1²/₃ oz) reduced-fat fetta
  cheese, crumbled

caramelised onion, artichoke & tomato pizzas

sweet potato & chilli bean wraps

SWEET POTATO & CHILLI BEAN WRAPS

4 (265 g/8½ oz) lavash slices

400 g (13 oz) prepared
  chargrilled sweet potato

50 g (1²/₃ oz) baby spinach

400 g (13 oz) can red kidney
  beans, drained weight
  300 g (10 oz)

1½ tablespoons chilli sauce

1 tablespoon chopped fresh
coriander (cilantro)

2 tablespoons light sour cream

1 Lay the lavash bread out on a flat surface. Arrange the sweet potato down the center of each and top with spinach leaves.

2 Put the beans, chilli sauce and coriander into a bowl and mix to combine.

3 Spoon the beans onto the sweet potato, top with the sour cream and roll up. Cook in a sandwich press until warmed through. Serves 4

per serve | fat 4 g | protein 14 g | carbohydrate 67 g | fibre 10.5 g | cholesterol 6.5 mg | energy 1530 kj (365 cal)

THAI SALAD CHICKEN BURGER

2 (680 g/1 lb 6 oz) skinless
  chicken breasts

olive oil spray

1 cup (90 g/3 oz) bean sprouts

1 large red chilli, seeded and
  cut into thin strips

2 tablespoons fresh mint leaves

1 carrot, sliced into ribbons
  with a vegetable peeler

1 tablespoon toasted
  sesame seeds

1 tablespoon lime juice

4 pieces (270 g/8²/₃ oz)
  wholemeal Turkish bread

50 g (1²/₃ oz) baby Asian
  green salad mix

1/3 cup (80 ml/2²/₃ fl oz) sweet
  chilli sauce

1 Trim the chicken of any excess fat or sinew. Cut the breasts in half through the center. Lightly spray a chargrill pan or barbecue with olive oil spray and cook the chicken over medium-high heat for 10-15 minutes or until tender.

2 Toss together the bean sprouts, chilli, mint, carrot, sesame seeds and lime juice.

3 Toast the Turkish bread until crisp and golden. Cover the bases with a little Asian salad mix and sprout salad, then top with slices of chicken.

4 Drizzle sweet chilli sauce over the chicken and top with lids of Turkish bread. Serves 4

per serve | fat 13 g | protein 44 g | carbohydrate 36.5 g | fibre 7 g | cholesterol 113 mg | energy 1845 kj (440 cal)

thai salad chicken burger

potato, pasta & onion tortilla

POTATO, PASTA & ONION TORTILLA

1 Cook the pasta in a large pan of rapidly boiling
water until al dente (cooked, but still with a bite to it).
Rinse under cold water to cool, then drain well.
2 Cook the potatoes, onion and garlic in the chicken
stock for about 5-10 minutes or until just soft.
Do not overcook or they will break up. Drain well.
3 Lightly spray a deep-sided non-stick fry pan
with olive oil spray. Arrange layers of the potato,
onion, garlic, basil and pasta in the pan.
4 Whisk the eggs and season with salt and pepper.
5 Pour the eggs over the potato layers and cook over
low-medium heat for 10 minutes or until the eggs are
set. Transfer the pan to a preheated grill and cook
under medium heat for 5 minutes or until the
tortilla comes away from the sides of the pan.
Serve cut into wedges with tomato salad. Serves 8

**per serve | fat 4.5 g | protein 8 g | carbohydrate 14 g
| fibre 1.5 g | cholesterol 140.5 mg | energy 535 kj (130 cal)**

100 g (3⅓ oz) rigatoni pasta
2 (250 g/8 oz) peeled potatoes,
   thickly sliced
1 medium brown onion,
   thinly sliced
2 cloves garlic, thinly sliced
2 cups (500 ml/16 fl oz)
   reduced-salt chicken stock
olive oil spray
2 tablespoons roughly chopped
   fresh basil leaves
6 eggs
salt and pepper

WARM POTATO, BEAN & TUNA SALAD

1 Put the potatoes in a large pan, cover with water
and cook until just tender. Drain and cool slightly
before cutting into thick slices.
2 Put the onion, beans, garlic, parsley, lemon juice,
stock and olive oil into a bowl and gently mix to
combine. Fold in the tuna and season with pepper.
3 Arrange potato slices on 4 plates and top with
the bean and tuna mixture. Serves 4

**per serve | fat 2 g | protein 21.5 g | carbohydrate 20 g
| fibre 5 g | cholesterol 34.5 mg | energy 800 kj (190 cal)**

500 g (1 lb) potatoes
1 red (Spanish) onion, thinly sliced
400 g (13 oz) can butter beans,
   drained weight 300 g (11 oz)
3 cloves garlic, crushed
¼ cup chopped fresh parsley
3 tablespoons lemon juice
¼ cup (60 ml/2 fl oz)
   reduced-salt chicken stock
1 tablespoon olive oil
400g (13 oz) can tuna in water,
   drained weight 260 g (8⅓ oz)
cracked black pepper

warm potato, bean & tuna salad

quick classic quiche

QUICK CLASSIC QUICHE

2 (100 g/3^{1}/$_{3}$ oz) flour tortillas

50 g (1^{2}/$_{3}$ oz) reduced-fat
  cheddar cheese, grated

2 eggs, lightly beaten

^{1}/$_{2}$ cup (125 ml/4 fl oz)
  reduced-fat cream

^{1}/$_{2}$ cup (125 ml/4 fl oz) skim
  or no-fat milk

100 g (3^{1}/$_{3}$ oz) 97% fat-free
  ham, chopped

3 spring onions (scallions), sliced

2 tablespoons chopped fresh chives

1 Preheat oven to 190°C (375°F/Gas 5).

2 Line the base of a 20 cm (8 in) pie dish with one flour tortilla. Cut the other tortilla into large triangles and arrange with the points to the center to fit around the pie dish. Sprinkle with half the cheese.

3 Whisk together all the remaining ingredients.

4 Pour the mixture over the tortillas and bake for 25-30 minutes or until the egg is just set. Serve with a garden salad. Serves 6

per serve | fat 10.5 g | protein 11 g | carbohydrate 11.5 g | fibre 1 g | cholesterol 92 mg | energy 755 kj (180 cal)

CHUNKY INDIAN VEGETABLE PATTIES

500 g (1 lb) peeled floury
  potatoes, roughly chopped

500 g (1 lb) peeled pumpkin,
  roughly chopped

2 teaspoons vegetable oil

1 medium brown onion, grated

2 tablespoons Madras curry paste

2 zucchini (courgette), grated

1 cup (95 g/3 oz) raw rolled oats

1 cup (70 g/2^{1}/$_{3}$ oz) fresh
  wholegrain breadcrumbs

olive oil spray

1 Cook the potatoes and pumpkin in a large pan of boiling water until tender. Drain well and return to the heat to absorb any excess liquid. Mash just enough to make a chunky mixture.

2 Heat the oil in a fry pan, add the onion and curry paste and cook over medium heat for 3 minutes or until the onion is soft.

3 Add the zucchini and cook for 5 minutes or until soft. Add to the potato and mix to combine. Remove from the heat and stir in oats and breadcrumbs.

4 Divide the mixture into 8 and form each portion into a round flat patty. Lightly spray the patties with olive oil spray and cook in a non-stick fry pan over medium-high heat until crisp and golden on both sides.

5 Serve the patties with warm wholemeal chapatis and Indian chutneys. Makes 8

per patty | fat 5 g | protein 6 g | carbohydrate 27 g | fibre 4 g | cholesterol 0 mg | energy 745 kj (180 cal)

chunky indian vegetable patties

DINNER

vermicelli nests with asian-style tuna

VERMICELLI NESTS WITH ASIAN-STYLE TUNA

150 g (5 oz) dried rice vermicelli
½ cup (15 g/½ oz) fresh
   coriander (cilantro) leaves
½ cup (15 g/½ oz) fresh
   mint leaves
juice and zest of 1 lime
1 large red chilli, seeded
   and cut into thin strips
1 tablespoon grated palm sugar
1 teaspoon sesame oil
1 bunch (255 g/8 oz) baby
   bok choy, washed
4 (630 g/1¼ lb) tuna steaks,
   cut in half crosswise
olive oil spray
2 tablespoons sweet chilli sauce

1 Put the vermicelli into a bowl, cover with boiling water and allow to stand for 10 minutes or until the noodles are soft. Rinse and drain well. Add the herbs, lime zest and chilli and toss to combine.
2 Add the lime juice, palm sugar and sesame oil to the noodles and toss to combine.
3 Steam the bok choy in a bamboo steamer or in the microwave until tender.
4 Cook the tuna steaks in a non-stick fry pan lightly sprayed with olive oil spray until cooked to your liking. Add the sweet chilli sauce to the pan, toss to coat the tuna in the sauce and cook for a minute or until sticky.
5 Serve mounds of noodles topped with tuna and bok choy to the side. Serves 4

per serve | fat 11 g | protein 43 g | carbohydrate 30.5 g | fibre 3 g | cholesterol 57 mg | energy 1665 kj (400 cal)

CHILLI CHICKEN, BASIL & CASHEW STIR FRY

2 teaspoons sunflower oil
500 g (1 lb) skinless chicken
   breasts, thinly sliced
4 spring onions (scallions), sliced
250 g (8 oz) broccoli,
   cut into florets
1 bunch (500 g/1 lb) Chinese
   broccoli, roughly chopped
3 tablespoons mild chilli sauce
1 tablespoon rice vinegar
2 tablespoons honey
¼ cup Thai basil leaves
¼ cup (35 g/1 oz) raw cashews

1 Heat the oil in a wok, add the chicken breasts and stir fry over a high heat until browned.
2 Add the spring onions and broccoli and stir fry for 3 minutes or until the broccoli is bright green.
3 Add the Chinese broccoli, chilli sauce, rice vinegar and honey and stir fry until the broccoli is cooked.
4 Remove from heat, add the basil and cashews. Serve with steamed jasmine rice. Serves 4

per serve | fat 14 g | protein 33.5 g | carbohydrate 18.5 g | fibre 7 g | cholesterol 82.5 mg | energy 1400 kj (335 cal)

chilli chicken, basil & cashew stir fry

thai fish balls with coriander salsa

THAI FISH BALLS WITH CORIANDER SALSA

1 Put the fish into a food processor and pulse to form a smooth paste. Transfer to a bowl and mix in the curry paste, beans, kaffir lime leaves and basil.
2 Divide the mixture into 12 roughly shaped balls. Cover and refrigerate for 30 minutes.
3 Preheat oven to 200°C (400°F/Gas 6).
4 Put the cucumber, coriander, fish sauce and chilli sauce into a bowl and mix to combine.
5 Heat the oil in a large fry pan, add the balls and cook over medium heat for 5 minutes on each side or until golden brown. Transfer to the oven and bake for 10 minutes or until cooked through.
6 Serve the fish balls with pots of salsa and steamed rice to the side. Serves 4

per serve | fat 10 g | protein 40.5 g | carbohydrate 5.5 g | fibre 3.5 g | cholesterol 110.5 mg | energy 1160 kj (275 cal)

750 g (1^1/$_2$ lb) skinless, boneless red fish fillets, roughly chopped
2 tablespoons green curry paste
50 g (1^2/$_3$ oz) snake beans, thinly sliced
4 kaffir lime leaves, finely shredded
6 Thai basil leaves, shredded
2 Lebanese cucumbers, unpeeled and diced
3 tablespoons chopped fresh coriander (cilantro)
2 tablespoons fish sauce
3 tablespoons sweet chilli sauce
2 teaspoons sunflower oil

CHARGRILLED CARAMEL PORK & APPLES WITH MASH

1 Put the pork chops and apples into a shallow non-metallic dish, pour over the combined kecap manis and balsamic vinegar, cover and marinate in the fridge for 15 minutes.
2 Cook the pork and apples on a lightly oiled chargrill pan or on the barbecue until tender.
3 Meanwhile, cook the potatoes in a pan of boiling water until tender and drain well. Add the stock and return to the heat to warm the stock.
4 Remove from heat and roughly mash. Season to taste with salt and pepper. Serves 4

per serve | fat 6 g | protein 32.5 g | carbohydrate 25.5 g | fibre 3.5 g | cholesterol 82 mg | energy 1220 kj (290 cal)

4 (560 g/1 lb 2 oz) lean pork loin chops
2 (330 g/11 oz) green apples, thickly sliced
2 tablespoons kecap manis (sweet soy sauce)
1 tablespoon balsamic vinegar
500 g (1 lb) peeled floury potatoes
1/4 cup (60 ml/2 fl oz) reduced-salt chicken stock
salt and pepper

chargrilled caramel pork & apples with mash

stir-fried pork, greens & noodles

STIR-FRIED PORK, GREENS & NOODLES

2 teaspoons vegetable oil

1 medium brown onion, thinly sliced

500 g (1 lb) lean pork fillet,
   thinly sliced

250 g (8 oz) broccoli, cut into florets

200 g (6½ oz) snowpeas, halved

200 g (6½ oz) green beans,
   halved

400 g (13 oz) fresh udon noodles

2 tablespoons sake

2 tablespoons mirin

3 tablespoons reduced-salt
   soy sauce

1 tablespoon caster sugar

1 Heat the oil in a wok, add onion and stir fry over medium heat for 3 minutes or until onion is soft.

2 Add the pork and stir fry for a few minutes until tender and cooked through.

3 Add the broccoli, snowpeas and beans. Stir fry for a few minutes or until bright green and just cooked.

4 Stir in the noodles and combined sake, mirin, soy and sugar. Stir fry for 3 minutes or until the noodles are soft and the sauce is thick and glossy. Serves 4

per serve | fat 6 g | protein 38 g | carbohydrate 35 g | fibre 7 g | cholesterol 118.5 mg | energy 1500 kj (360 cal)

PENNE WITH ROAST PUMPKIN, FENNEL & GOAT'S CHEESE

500 g (1 lb) peeled pumpkin,
   thickly sliced

1 medium (220 g/7 oz) fennel
   bulb, cored and thinly sliced

8 Roma tomatoes, halved

1 head garlic

olive oil spray

500 g (1 lb) penne pasta

¼ cup small fresh basil leaves

50 g (1²/₃ oz) goat's cheese

1 Preheat oven to 200°C (400°F/Gas 6).

2 Put the pumpkin, fennel, tomatoes and garlic onto a baking tray, spray lightly with olive oil spray and bake for 40 minutes or until the vegetables are soft.

3 Cook the pasta in a large pan of rapidly boiling water until al dente (cooked, but still with a bite to it). Drain well.

4 Return the pasta to the pan and add the vegetables, basil and goat's cheese. Gently toss to combine and serve hot. Serves 6

per serve | fat 3.5 g | protein 14 g | carbohydrate 65.5 g | fibre 7 g | cholesterol 3.5 mg | energy 1475 kj (350 cal)

penne with roast pumpkin, fennel & goat's cheese

tofu & mushrooms with japanese rice

TOFU & MUSHROOMS WITH JAPANESE RICE

1 Put the rice into a pan and add 1 1/2 cups (375 ml/12 fl oz) cold water. Bring to the boil and cook over medium heat for 10 minutes or until tunnels appear in the rice. Reduce heat to low, cover and cook for 5 minutes more or until the rice is soft. Stir through the nori just before serving.
2 Put the dried shiitake into a bowl, cover with 1/2 cup (125 ml/4 fl oz) boiling water and stand for 10 minutes or until soft. Reserve the soaking liquid.
3 Heat the oil in a wok, add the tofu and cook over medium-high heat for 3-5 minutes or until the tofu is golden. Remove and drain on absorbent paper.
4 Add the soaked mushrooms, spring onions and fresh shiitake to the wok and stir fry over high heat until the mushrooms are golden brown. Add the enoki and cook for 1 minute more.
5 Stir in the combined mushroom soaking liquid, mirin, soy and sugar. Cook, stirring constantly, until the sauce thickens slightly.
6 Serve tofu with the mushrooms and broth and steamed rice in a bowl to the side. Serves 4
per serve | **fat 7.5 g** | **protein 17 g** | **carbohydrate 50 g** | **fibre 5 g** | **cholesterol 0 mg** | **energy 1410 kj (335 cal)**

1 cup (205 g/6 1/2 oz) Japanese rice
1 (5 g/1/6 oz) sheet nori seaweed, finely shredded
50 g (1 2/3 oz) dried small shiitake mushrooms
2 teaspoons sunflower oil
300 g (10 oz) firm silken tofu, cut into 2.5 cm (1 in) cubes
3 spring onions (scallions), sliced
200 g (6 1/2 oz) fresh shiitake mushrooms, sliced
100 g (3 1/3 oz) enoki mushrooms
1/4 cup (60 ml/2 fl oz) mirin
1/3 cup (80 ml/2 2/3 fl oz) reduced-salt soy sauce
1 tablespoon caster sugar

CHICKEN & SAFFRON RISOTTO

2 cups (500 ml/16 fl oz)
reduced-salt chicken stock

2 cups (500 ml/16 fl oz)
tomato puree

1 cup (250 ml/8 fl oz) white wine

pinch saffron threads

20 g (²/₃ oz) reduced-fat
polyunsaturated margarine

1 tablespoon olive oil

2 cloves garlic, crushed

1 medium brown onion,
finely chopped

500 g (1 lb) skinless, boneless
chicken thigh fillets, chopped

½ teaspoon cayenne pepper

1 medium red capsicum (bell
pepper), cut into cubes

1 medium green capsicum (bell
pepper), cut into cubes

2 cups (410 g/14 oz) arborio rice

cracked black pepper

¼ cup (20 g/²/₃ oz) finely
grated parmesan cheese

2 tablespoons chopped fresh
flat-leaf parsley

sea salt

1 Preheat oven to 160°C (310°F/Gas 2½).

2 Put the stock, tomato puree, wine and saffron into a pan. Bring to the boil, reduce heat and keep at simmering point for about 10 minutes while preparing the rest of the recipe.

3 Put the margarine and oil in a large ovenproof casserole dish. Add the garlic and onion and cook over medium heat for 3 minutes or until onion is soft.

4 Add the chicken and cook for 5 minutes or until browned. Add the cayenne and capsicum and cook for about 3 minutes or until soft.

5 Stir in the rice and cook, stirring constantly, for 1 minute or until the rice is coated with the oil. Add the simmering liquid and season with cracked black pepper. Cook uncovered on the middle shelf of the oven for 30 minutes.

6 Remove the risotto from the oven, stir in parmesan and cook for 15 minutes longer or until the rice is soft. Stir through the parsley and season with salt and extra black pepper. Serves 6

per serve | fat 12.5 g | protein 24.5 g | carbohydrate 61.5 g | fibre 3 g | cholesterol 76 mg | energy 2040 kj (485 cal)

chicken & saffron risotto

roast chicken with tandoori-baked vegetables

ROAST CHICKEN WITH TANDOORI-BAKED VEGETABLES

1 Put the garlic, paprika, cumin, cinnamon and yoghurt into a large, shallow non-metallic dish. Season generously with salt and pepper.

2 Add the chicken (skin on or off - see analysis below) and turn to coat in the yoghurt. Cover and refrigerate overnight if possible.

3 Preheat oven to 200°C (400°F/Gas 6). Transfer the chicken to a large baking dish and baste it generously all over with the yoghurt.

4 Cut the vegetables into large pieces. Toss together with tandoori paste and arrange around the chicken.

5 Roast the chicken on a lightly oiled rack for 1¼ hours or until tender, turning the vegetables a couple of times during cooking. If the chicken skin is left on and starts to brown too much, cover with lightly greased foil. Serves 6

per serve (skin on) | fat 18.5 g | protein 28 g | carbohydrate 21 g | fibre 4.5 g | cholesterol 111 mg | energy 1530 kj (365 cal)

per serve (skin off) | fat 10.5 g | protein 29 g | carbohydrate 21 g | fibre 4.5 g | cholesterol 91.5 mg | energy 1250 kj (300 cal)

2 cloves garlic, crushed

2 teaspoons sweet paprika

1 teaspoon ground cumin

1 teaspoon ground cinnamon

1 cup (250 ml/8 fl oz) reduced-fat Greek-style yoghurt

salt and pepper

1.5 kg (3 lb) whole chicken

1 kg (2 lb) prepared roasting vegetables (potatoes, pumpkin, parsnips, onions)

2 tablespoons tandoori paste

EASY PUMPKIN & SPINACH LASAGNE

1 kg (2 lb) peeled pumpkin,
   thickly sliced
olive oil spray
300 g (10 oz) low-fat
   ricotta cheese
2 tablespoons skim or no-fat milk
6 (280 g/9 oz) fresh
   lasagne sheets
100 g (3⅓ oz) baby spinach
8 Roma tomatoes, thickly sliced
¼ cup small fresh basil leaves
2 tablespoons balsamic vinegar
1 cup (250 ml/8 fl oz) tomato
   pasta sauce
40 g (1⅓ oz) reduced-fat
   mozzarella, grated

1 Preheat oven to 200°C (400°F/Gas 6).
2 Put the pumpkin on 2 non-stick baking
trays, spray lightly with olive oil spray and
bake for 30 minutes or until soft.
3 Put the ricotta and milk into a bowl and mix.
4 Place 1½ sheets of the lasagne into a
20 cm x 30 cm (8 in x 12 in) ovenproof dish.
Top with half of the pumpkin, spread with half
the ricotta and top with half the spinach.
5 Top with another layer of lasagne and half the
tomato slices, scatter half the basil leaves over
the top and drizzle with half the balsamic vinegar.
Repeat the layers, finishing with a layer of tomato
passata, tomatoes, basil and vinegar.
6 Sprinkle mozzarella over the top and bake
for 40 minutes or until the lasagne sheets are
tender and the cheese is golden. Serves 8

per serve | fat 5 g | protein 11.5 g | carbohydrate 22.5 g
| fibre 4 g | cholesterol 19.5 mg | energy 755 kj (180 cal)

easy pumpkin & spinach lasagne

lamb skewers with mediterranean salad

LAMB SKEWERS WITH MEDITERRANEAN SALAD

1 Thread the lamb onto small bamboo skewers
that have been soaking in water for 30 minutes.
Put into a shallow non-metallic dish with tomatoes.
2 Whisk together the oregano, lemon juice, garlic
and olive oil and pour over the lamb and tomatoes.
Marinate for 30 minutes in the fridge.
3 Cook the lamb and tomatoes on a barbecue flat
plate or in a large fry pan for about 5-10 minutes
or until cooked to your liking.
4 Put the couscous into a bowl, pour over 2 cups
(500 ml/16 fl oz) boiling water and allow to stand
for 10 minutes or until the liquid is absorbed.
5 Stir in onion and spoon the couscous onto plates.
Top with the rocket, cucumber, tomato and lamb
skewers and scatter fetta over the top. Serve with
lemon wedges. Serves 4

per serve | fat 11 g | protein 27 g | carbohydrate 39 g
| fibre 2.5 g | cholesterol 58.5 mg | energy 1535 kj (365 cal)

300 g (10 oz) lean lamb loin,
   cut into 2.5 cm (1 in) cubes
4 Roma tomatoes, halved
   lengthwise
1 teaspoon chopped fresh
   oregano leaves
2 tablespoons lemon juice
2 cloves garlic, crushed
2 teaspoons olive oil
1 cup (185 g/6 oz) couscous
1 red (Spanish) onion, thinly sliced
100 g (3⅓ oz) baby rocket
   (arugula)
1 Lebanese cucumber, unpeeled
   and thinly sliced
50 g (1⅔ oz) reduced-fat fetta
   cheese, crumbled

SPICY PASTA & BEAN BAKE

200 g (6½ oz) rigatoni pasta

1 egg, lightly beaten

½ cup (125 ml/4 fl oz) skim
   or no-fat milk

2 teaspoons olive oil

1 medium brown onion, finely
   chopped

500 g (1 lb) lean beef mince

¼ teaspoon cayenne pepper

1 medium red capsicum
   (bell pepper), chopped

400 g (13 oz) can chopped tomatoes

2 tablespoons tomato paste

400 g (13 oz) can red kidney
   beans, drained weight
      300 g (10 oz)

1 tablespoon red wine vinegar

1 teaspoon brown sugar

⅓ cup (40 g/1⅓ oz) grated
   reduced-fat cheddar cheese

1 Preheat oven to 200°C (400°F/Gas 6).

2 Cook the pasta in a large pan of rapidly boiling water until al dente (cooked, but still with a bite to it). Drain well.

3 Whisk together the egg and milk. Heat oil in a large fry pan, add the onion and cook over medium heat for 5 minutes or until soft.

4 Add the mince and cayenne and cook until the mince begins to brown. Add the capsicum, tomatoes and tomato paste and bring to the boil. Reduce heat, cover and simmer for 15 minutes.

5 Add beans, vinegar and sugar and heat through.

6 Spoon the pasta into a 20 cm (8 in) round pie dish and pour over the egg mixture. Top with beef mixture and sprinkle with cheese. Bake for about 30 minutes or until the cheese is golden. Serve cut into wedges with salad. Serves 6

per serve I **fat 10 g** I **protein 29 g** I **carbohydrate 36 g** I **fibre 6 g** I **cholesterol 78 mg** I **energy 1480 kj (355 cal)**

spicy pasta & bean bake

SWEET THINGS

berry bombes alaska

BERRY BOMBES ALASKA

300g (10 oz) fresh or frozen
  mixed berries
4 scoops (90 g/3 oz) reduced-fat
  vanilla ice cream
3 egg whites
¾ cup (180 g/6 oz) caster sugar

1 Preheat oven to 230°C (450°F/Gas 8).
2 Divide the berries equally among 4 x ½ cup (125 ml/4 fl oz) capacity ramekins. Top with a scoop of ice cream. Leave the ramekins in the freezer while making the meringue.
3 Whisk the egg whites in a clean, dry bowl for 2-3 minutes or until soft peaks form. Continue whisking vigorously while gradually adding the sugar until the mixture is stiff and glossy.
4 Remove the ramekins from the freezer and place on a baking tray. Spread the meringue evenly over the tops of the ice cream, making sure it meets the edge of each ramekin.
5 Bake for 2-3 minutes or until the meringue tops are golden but the ice cream remains frozen. Serve immediately. Serves 4

per serve | fat 1.5 g | protein 5 g | carbohydrate 53.5 g | fibre 1.5 g | cholesterol 5.5 mg | energy 995 kj (240 cal)

SPICED PLUM BREAD & BUTTER PUDDING

1 (500 g/1 lb) Turkish bread
800 g (1 lb 10 oz) can pitted
  dark plums, drained weight
  550 g (1 lb 2 oz)
3 eggs, lightly beaten
2 cups (500 ml/16 fl oz) skim
  or no-fat milk
1 teaspoon mixed spice
3 tablespoons raw sugar

1 Preheat oven to 180°C (350°F/Gas 4). Lightly grease a 6 cup (1.5 litres/48 fl oz) capacity ovenproof dish.
2 Cut the Turkish bread in half through the center. Cut the halves into 15 cm (6 in) squares, then cut each square into triangles.
3 Layer the bread and plums into the prepared dish.
4 Put the eggs and milk into a jug and whisk to combine. Pour over the bread and sprinkle with the combined mixed spiced and raw sugar. Bake for 35-40 minutes or until custard is just set. Serves 6

per serve | fat 3.5 g | protein 13 g | carbohydrate 67 g | fibre 3.5 g | cholesterol 96.5 mg | energy 1465 kj (350 cal)

spiced plum bread & butter pudding

orange & poppy seed cornmeal cake

ORANGE & POPPY SEED CORNMEAL CAKE

1 Preheat oven to 180°C (350°F/Gas 4). Lightly grease and line a 20 cm (8 in) spring form tin.
2 Put the eggs and sugar into a bowl and beat with electric beaters on high for about 5 minutes or until the mixture is thick and pale.
3 Gently fold in the 3 teaspoons of orange zest, cardamom, 1/2 cup orange juice, cornmeal, poppy seeds and flour. Pour the mixture into the tin and bake for 30 minutes or until a skewer comes out clean when inserted into the center.
4 To make the syrup, put 1 tablespoon of zest, 1 cup of orange juice and 1/2 cup sugar into a small pan and stir over a low heat until the sugar dissolves. Bring to the boil and cook over high heat for 10 minutes or until syrupy. Pour half the hot syrup over the hot cake while still in the tin. Serve slices of cake drizzled with the remaining syrup. Serves 10

per serve | fat 4 g | protein 5 g | carbohydrate 42.5 g | fibre 1.5 g | cholesterol 71.5 mg | energy 925 kj (220 cal)

4 eggs
1/2 cup (125 g/4 oz) caster sugar
3 teaspoons grated orange zest
1 teaspoon ground cardamom
1/2 cup (125 ml/4 fl oz) fresh orange juice
1/2 cup (75 g/2 1/2 oz) fine cornmeal (polenta)
1/4 cup (40 g/1 1/3 oz) poppy seeds
1 cup (125 g/4 oz) self-raising flour
1 tablespoon orange zest, extra
1 cup (250 ml/8 fl oz) fresh orange juice, extra
1/2 cup (125 g/4 oz) caster sugar, extra

CHOCOLATE MARSHMALLOW BROWNIES

1 Preheat oven to 180°C (350°F/Gas 4). Lightly grease and line a 20 cm (8 in) square cake tin.
2 Sift the flour and cocoa into a bowl and stir in the sugar, marshmallows and chocolate.
3 Whisk together the yoghurt, eggs, vanilla and oil. Add to the dry ingredients and mix to combine.
4 Pour the mixture into the prepared tin and bake for 25-30 minutes. Cool in the tin before cutting into even squares. Makes 16

per brownie | fat 3 g | protein 3 g | carbohydrate 29 g | fibre 0.5 g | cholesterol 25 mg | energy 625 kj (150 cal)

105 g (3 1/2 oz) self-raising flour
1/3 cup (45 g/1 1/2 oz) cocoa powder
1 cup (250 g/8 oz) caster sugar
100 g (3 1/3 oz) white marshmallows, roughly chopped
50 g (1 2/3 oz) milk chocolate melts or buttons
1/2 cup (125 ml/4 fl oz) reduced-fat plain yoghurt
2 eggs, lightly beaten
1 teaspoon vanilla essence
1 tablespoon vegetable oil

chocolate marshmallow brownies

mango meringue praline ice cream

MANGO MERINGUE PRALINE ICE CREAM

1 cup (250 g/8 oz) sugar
¼ cup (25 g/1 oz) flaked almonds
450 g (15 oz) mango 97% fat-free
    frozen fruit dessert
500 g (1 lb) low-fat vanilla
    ice cream
50 g (1²/₃ oz) pre-baked
    meringue, lightly crushed

1 Put the sugar and ½ cup (125 ml/4 fl oz) water into a small pan. Stir over low heat until the sugar dissolves, bring to the boil and cook without stirring until the sugar turns a dark golden caramel colour.
2 Add the almonds and swirl to combine.
3 Pour the caramel out onto a baking tray lined with non-stick baking paper and leave to set. Roughly crush all but ⅓ of the praline, breaking the remaining praline into large pieces for garnish.
4 Put the mango dessert, ice cream, meringue and crushed praline into a large bowl and gently stir to combine. Freeze until firm. Serve bowls of ice cream decorated with reserved praline. Serves 8

per serve | fat 3.5 g | protein 2.5 g | carbohydrate 55.5 g | fibre 0.5 g | cholesterol 3 mg | energy 1105 kj (265 cal)

RHUBARB & YOGHURT BRULEE

1 bunch rhubarb, leaves discarded
    and cut into 5 cm (2 in) pieces,
    trimmed weight 330 g (11 oz)
1 vanilla bean, halved lengthwise
½ cup (125 g/4 oz) caster sugar
2 cups (500 ml/16 fl oz) reduced-
fat Greek-style natural yoghurt
1 cup (250 g/8 oz) sugar

1 Put the rhubarb and vanilla into a pan and add ¼ cup (60 ml/2 fl oz) water. Cover and cook over low-medium heat for 3-5 minutes or until the rhubarb is just tender. Do not overcook or the rhubarb will collapse. Add sugar and stir gently to dissolve. Cool slightly, then discard the vanilla bean.
2 Divide the rhubarb equally among 4 x ½ cup (125 ml/4 fl oz) capacity heatproof glasses and top with yoghurt and any rhubarb syrup.
3 Place the sugar in a small pan and cook over low-medium heat without stirring until the sugar dissolves and starts to turn a deep caramel colour. Carefully pour the hot caramel over the yoghurt. Allow to set before serving. Serves 4

per serve | fat 2.5 g | protein 7 g | carbohydrate 106.5 g | fibre 1.5 g | cholesterol 12.5 mg | energy 1935 kj (460 cal)

rhubarb & yoghurt brulee

BAKED CHEESECAKE WITH STRAWBERRIES

15 g (½ oz) reduced-fat
  polyunsaturated margarine
25 g (1 oz) digestive biscuits,
  crushed
500 g (1 lb) low-fat ricotta cheese,
  drained of all excess liquid
250 g (8 oz) light, reduced-fat soft
  cream cheese, chopped
½ cup (125 g/4 oz) caster sugar
1 teaspoon vanilla essence
1 teaspoon grated lemon zest
250 g (8 oz) strawberries, halved
2 tablespoons maple syrup

1 Preheat oven to 160°C (310°F/Gas 2½).
2 Grease the base and side of a 20 cm (8 in) spring form tin with melted margarine, add the biscuit crumbs and tilt and turn the tin to coat the base and sides with crumbs.
3 Put the ricotta into a food processor and process for 5 minutes or until smooth and creamy.
4 Add the cream cheese, sugar, vanilla and lemon zest and process for 2 minutes or until smooth.
5 Pour the mixture into the tin and place on two long sheets of aluminium foil. Fold the foil around the side of the tin to waterproof the base. Leave the surface of the cheesecake uncovered.
6 Place the tin into a baking dish and pour in enough water to come halfway up the side of the tin. Bake for 45-50 minutes or until just set. Remove from the baking dish and water immediately, discard the foil and cool in the tin, then refrigerate. Serve topped with strawberries and maple syrup. Serves 8
per serve | fat 12 g | protein 10 g | carbohydrate 23 g | fibre 1 g | cholesterol 42.5 mg | energy 990 kj (235 cal)

TROPICAL FRUIT RICE DESSERT

⅓ cup (70 g/2⅓ oz) arborio rice
3 cups (750 ml/24 fl oz) skim
  or no-fat milk
⅓ cup (60 g/2 oz) palm sugar,
  grated
1 vanilla bean, halved lengthwise
150 g (5 oz) peeled red papaya
250 g (8 oz) peeled pineapple
90 g (3 oz) peeled guava
1 medium kiwifruit
juice and zest of 1 lime

1 Put the rice, milk, sugar and vanilla bean into a pan. Stir over low heat until sugar dissolves. Bring to the boil, reduce heat and simmer for 1 hour, stirring occasionally, or until the rice is tender.
2 Remove the vanilla bean.
3 Chop the fruit into chunks and place in a bowl with the juice and zest. Mix gently to combine. Serve bowls of rice topped with fruit. Serves 4
per serve | fat 0.5 g | protein 9.5 g | carbohydrate 48.5 g | fibre 4.5 g | cholesterol 6 mg | energy 1000 kj (240 cal)

baked cheesecake with strawberries

tropical fruit rice dessert

turkish delight pastries with fragrant watermelon

TURKISH DELIGHT PASTRIES WITH FRAGRANT WATERMELON

¼ cup (60 g/2 oz) caster sugar

1 cup (250 ml/8 fl oz) water

juice and zest of 1 small lemon

1 teaspoon rosewater

1 tablespoon fresh mint leaves

400 g (13 oz) watermelon,
   cut into small triangles

4 sheets filo (phyllo) pastry

20 g (²/₃ oz) reduced-fat
   polyunsaturated margarine

200 g (6½ oz) plain Turkish
   delight, chopped

icing sugar, to serve

1 Put the sugar, water, lemon juice, zest and rosewater into a pan and stir over low heat until sugar dissolves. Bring to the boil, then simmer for 10 minutes. Remove from the heat and cool slightly. Pour syrup over the mint leaves and watermelon and stand at room temperature for 30 minutes.

2 Preheat oven to 200°C (400°F/Gas 6).

3 Brush 1 sheet of filo pastry with melted margarine, then top with another sheet. Set aside. Do the same with the remaining 2 sheets of pastry.

4 Cut both pastry squares into 4 pieces lengthwise to make 8 even strips. Put a few pieces of Turkish delight onto the end of a strip of pastry, fold the edges in and roll up to form a small cigar-shaped pastry. Repeat with the remaining pastry and Turkish delight. Place the 8 pastries onto a non-stick baking tray and brush lightly with margarine.

5 Cook for 15-20 minutes or until crisp and golden.

6 Serve warm pastries lightly dusted with icing sugar and watermelon to the side. Serves 4

per serve | fat 3 g | protein 2 g | carbohydrate 63 g | fibre 1 g | cholesterol 0 mg | energy 1175 kj (280 cal)

BANANA & PASSIONFRUIT OPEN TRIFLE

400 g (13 oz) low-fat or light
   vanilla fromage frais

½ cup (125 ml/4 fl oz)
   low-fat vanilla custard

16 thin (190 g/6¼ oz)
   sponge finger biscuits

2 (200 g/6½ oz) bananas, sliced

½ cup (125 ml/4 fl oz)
   passionfruit pulp

1 Put the fromage frais into a bowl and fold through the custard until smooth.

2 Arrange the sponge finger biscuits on 4 plates, top each with a dollop of the custard mixture and finish with banana and passionfruit pulp. Serves 4

per serve | fat 3 g | protein 15 g | carbohydrate 55.5 g | fibre 6 g | cholesterol 80 mg | energy 1325 kj (315 cal)

banana & passionfruit open trifle

READING FOOD LABELS IN AUSTRALIA & NEW ZEALAND

Reading the nutrition information on food labels while shopping is very helpful for selecting low-fat foods. However, you need to be able to interpret the information on the food labels correctly. In Australia and New Zealand, food manufacturers are required by law to list the ingredients in a product on its packaging in order of decreasing weight, so the ingredient that makes up most of the product is listed first. If a product's packaging shows a nutrition information panel, the main nutrients in the food must be listed for an average serve of the food, and per 100 grams or 100 ml of the food. For products that are sold in fixed portions, such as a snack bar or a small tub of yoghurt, it is useful to compare the amount of fat per serve of each food. For products that are sold in larger amounts, rather than individual portions, such as breakfast cereals, margarine, large cartons of milk and large tubs of yoghurt, it is more useful to compare the amount of fat per 100 grams or 100 ml. Some products also have nutrient claims on their food labels, such as 'low-fat' or 'lite', and these can be confusing on their own. You will need to double-check the nutrition information panel to be able to determine just how accurate some of these claims are: a 25 % reduced-fat hard cheese may still contain a lot more fat than cottage cheese, and lite margarine is still a high-fat food.

FAT-RELATED NUTRIENT CLAIMS ON FOOD LABELS

1 | **Reduced-fat** foods must have at least 25% less fat than the regular version, but may still contain significant fat and calories.

2 | **Low-fat or low in fat** products must not contain more than 3 grams (solid foods) or 1.5 grams (liquids) of fat per 100 grams.

3 | **Light or lite** is a confusing claim which can refer to a product's fat content or its lighter colour, such as lite olive oil, which is lighter in colour than virgin olive oil but still contains 100% fat. It can also refer to a product's taste, texture, salt or sugar content. So always check the fat content listed in the nutrition information panel. If the product is labelled 'lite' due to its fat content, then it must also qualify as a reduced- or low-fat food.

4 | **X% fat-free** foods should also be low-fat foods with less than 1.5-3% fat, but some manufacturers are still using this claim on fattier foods, such as 95% fat-free biscuits or 90% fat-free cheese. A food that is 90% fat-free hasn't had 90% of its fat removed − it contains 10% fat. So make sure you double-check the fat content in the nutrition information panel.

5 | **Cholesterol-free** products must not contain more than 3 mg of cholesterol per 100 grams and should also be low in fat or low in saturated fat. Some low saturated fat foods - including avocados, vegetable oils and polyunsaturated margarine - can still be high in total fat.

Publisher Jody Vassallo
General manager Claire Connolly
Recipes & styling Jody Vassallo
Photographer Ben Dearnley
Home economist Angela Treggoning
Recipe tester Camilla Jessop
Props stylist Melissa Singer
Designer Nicole Vonwiller
Editor Lynelle Scott-Aitken
Consulting nutritionist Dr Susanna Holt

STYLING CREDITS:
Country Road (03) 9267 1400
David Jones 13 33 57
Lincraft (03) 9525 8770
Made in Japan (02) 9410 3799
Mud Australia (02) 9518 0220
Orson & Blake (02) 9326 1155
Royal Doulton (02) 9499 1904
Spotlight (03) 9690 8899
Tomkin (02) 9319 2993
Villeroy & Boch (02) 9975 3099
Wheel & Barrow (02) 9413 9530
© **Recipes** Jody Vassallo 2002
© **Photography** Ben Dearnley
© **Series design** Fortiori Publishing

PUBLISHED BY FORTIORI PUBLISHING:
PO Box 126 Nunawading BC
Victoria 3110 Australia
Phone: 61 3 9872 3855
Fax: 61 3 9872 5454
salesenquiries@fortiori.com.au
www.fortiori.com.au

order direct on (03) 9872 3855

Printed by McPherson's Printing Group.
Printed in Australia.

ISBN 0 9581609 1 0

DISCLAIMER: The nutritional information listed under each recipe does not include the nutrient content of garnishes or any accompaniments not listed in specific quantities in the ingredient list. The nutritional information for each recipe is an estimate only, and may vary depending on the brand of ingredients used, and due to natural biological variations in the composition of natural foods such as meat, fish, fruit and vegetables. The nutritional information was calculated by a qualified dietitian using FoodWorks dietary analysis software (Version 3, Xyris Software Pty Ltd, Highgate Hill, Queensland, Australia) based on the Australian food composition tables and food manufacturers' data. Where not specified, ingredients are always analysed as average or medium, not small or large. All recipes were analysed using 59 g eggs.

IMPORTANT: Those who might be at risk from the effects of salmonella food poisoning (the elderly, pregnant women, young children and those suffering from immune deficiency diseases) should consult their general practitioner about consuming raw or undercooked eggs.